Video Marke[ ] Creating Actionable Online Videos, Hardworking Video Ads, and more

WEYK GLOBAL BOOK SERIES
Zachary Lukasiewicz

ISBN:9781713017516

CONTENTS

WEYK GLOBAL MEDIA
Lincoln, Nebraska
www.weykglobal.com

Related Courses & Workshops: WeykGlobal.com

LinkedIn: linkedin.com/in/zdrake2013

More about the author: weykglobal.com/leadership

Please send errors, comments, and speaking inquiries

to hey@weykglobal.com

The goal in releasing this book series is to help narrow the gap between professional marketers and industry newcomers. The idea here is to provide necessary information to passionate individuals to make their business dreams a reality. Our marketing materials - including our courses and workshops - are all aligned on this front.

For Whom Is This Book Intended?

This book is meant for start-ups and small businesses that lack marketing-savvy staff but have a need to intelligently expand the reach of their goods or services. These companies may not have the budget to hire external marketing help, and may also find traditional Google tools to be intimidating. We seek to educate and demystify the online marketplace for these organizations.

What Does It Do?

Using a series of lessons, case studies, and quizzes (if you opt for our online courses), this book and its entire series guides you through 3-5 minute story-based chapters on search marketing, content marketing, PR & Media and more. All in all, we cover eighteen different topics. The lessons in this book are heavy on strategy and light on execution. Though this book helps readers differentiate between marketing tactics and identify the best strategies for different businesses, it does not go so far as to provide a detailed walk-through of execution using Google tools. That said, it certainly provides enough information to begin taking steps in the right direction.

How Does It Do It?

This book handles dry topics well, making consistency paramount. This keeps readers engaged in the lessons, with no time to lose focus. There are also notes about various courses and workshops to help reinforce the takeaways. Reviewing all of the chapters takes less than 45 minutes. As a digital marketing instructor for Growth (X) Academy, I integrate these essentials into my lessons on search marketing and content marketing in order to reinforce concepts.

Use Video Content to Create a Community

Why is video important for my marketing efforts?

How can I create engaging video content?

How can I use video content to build a loyal audience?

These days, it seems that there is so much video content that it's hard to get viewers' attention.

When a brand makes a video channel, it's not only competing with other brands, but also with everything else that lives online. Still, some brands seem to have a loyal following. So, what content gets people engaged?

Let's say an auto company launches an online video series for a new hybrid car. They repurpose a series of stunning ads from their TV campaign that highlights the car's high-powered performance and its low price.

They post the ads on the brand's online channels, share them on social media, and wait. But 2 weeks later there are few likes, shares, and comments.

Why didn't the videos get any traction?

No matter what kind of videos you create, make sure they're consistent with your brand voice.

This means your content should be honest, genuine, and true to your brand. Consumers are savvy. They won't engage if they feel the content is inauthentic or forced.

For example, if you run a fast food chain, making a high quality cooking show video series might not resonate with your audience.

TIP

You can save a lot of time and money by looking at what your competitors and independent creators in your brand category are doing.

Try and figure out what works and what doesn't. You can get good insights just by looking at the comment section.

Video content works when it's about a subject or interest that both your target audience and brand care about.

That sounds easy if you're an airline ("woohoo, travel"), but what if you're a dishwashing liquid brand? ("boohoo, cleaning up.")

The key is to get specific. Find an element in your product or service that your audience finds useful or entertaining.

For instance, people often go online to look for videos that offer tips and tricks, so you can make a series of how-to videos, anything from "the 8 things you can clean in your dishwasher," to a cooking show.

By focusing on these themes, you're not only offering practical value to the audience, but the dishwashing liquid becomes a natural part of the narrative.

LISTEN UP

Not everyone is interested in your entire video library. Some just might want to see a specific video.

Think how your content works for those interested in the entire theme of your channel, and those who are interested in just an individual video.

Got your idea? Now it's time to make some videos. So lights, camera...wait up. Before you start filming, there's a few things to consider about production.

One-hit viral videos are great, but they're not something that will sustain an audience's attention in the long run. Instead, aim to create a consistent video series to maintain and increase engagement with your audience over time.

This means that you should upload your videos on a regular

schedule. Imagine your favorite TV show airs an episode today, and then 2 weeks later, and then only after a month...by then it will most likely not be your favorite show anymore.

Invite guest stars to widen the appeal of the content and attract new audiences. They don't have to be A-list celebrities. You can feature bloggers or key influencers in your industry – anyone who can present your brand in a positive light.

Decide how many episodes to produce, and how long the content will be relevant on the channel. A series can only run so long before the concept gets old, so think what future content will help to maintain audience engagement.

Get the most out of your video production. All those lights, camera, action, and people don't come cheap. Try and shoot multiple episodes/videos at a time to maximize resources.

TOOLS

To get eyes on your videos, publish on popular online video platforms, such as YouTube or Vimeo.

You can also embed your videos on your social media channels.

Once you have your content ready, it's time to launch. But before you hit "publish," lay the groundwork.

Before people see your video, they see a thumbnail. It's helpful to think of a thumbnail like a movie poster. It should be eye-catching, show the most exciting moment in the video, and look good on desktop and mobile.

The first thing people read is your title, so come up with a catchy name for your video to draw them in. Research keywords and tags that are popular with your audience to make sure your titles can be found easily on search engines.

Viewers see the top 2 sentences in your video description area before clicking to see more. This is prime real estate to highlight your call to action (CTA), like a link to your website, social channels, or related videos or playlists.

Show you're listening by replying to comments. Treat your most active users like VIPs. Highlight their comments, give them rewards, and invite them to appear in your videos.

In the end, what people value most is entertainment, utility, and personal interaction. By engaging with them and talking about what's important to them, you increase your brand affinity and build a loyal audience.

KEY TAKEAWAYS

1. Video content is about increasing brand affinity and creating conversations with your target audience.

2. You can create compelling content but finding themes that your audience is interested in.

3. By engaging with your audience and asking for their opinions and comments, you can build a loyal audience.

Skip the Ordinary: Create Engaging Online Video Ads

Why do I need to create engaging online video ads?

How can I make sure my online video ads are entertaining and memorable?

How can I test my online video ads to see which ones perform best?

Before we start talking about online video ads, let's try a quick exercise: Imagine you're on the way to the store to buy eggs when you notice a street musician.

You're drawn in by the quality of the music and the crowd, so you stop to listen. Before you know it, you've heard 5 songs.

Successful online video ads are just like that street musician. They convince someone who stumbles across them to stay and watch, instead of immediately continuing on to their destination.

Of course, not every online video ad will be able to stop viewers from hitting the "skip ad" button. Certain types of ads have a higher chance of drawing viewers in.

So what type of video ads attract the most attention?

There isn't one definitive way to make great online video ads. That's because good ads use online platforms in surprising and creative ways.

However, there is one starter step you should take before coming up with ideas for online video ads: Think about how you want these ads to help you reach your business goals.

The goal of your video ads could be increasing brand awareness, driving sales, or building a loyal and vocal following. Having a clear goal helps you narrow in on the emotions you want your online video ads to evoke.

Clear goals also help you figure out what action viewers should take, like visiting your online store, or sharing the ad on their social media accounts.

LISTEN UP

Depending on the scope of the project and your resources, you might consider using a digital agency that specializes in online advertising. But, if you have a smaller budget, you might hire freelancers with expertise in shooting, editing, and analyzing the results of online video ads.

After you've decided what your goal is and found an agency or freelancer, it's time to brainstorm some internet-breaking ideas.

While the content of your online video ads should be original and unique to your brand, you can rely on some tried and true elements to help make your videos more entertaining and engaging.

First, if it's appropriate, consider using humor. That's because humorous ads usually get more views than other types of ads. Obviously, being funny isn't right for every brand, so use it wisely.

Star power can also go a long way. Partner with social influencers or celebrities to get your audience interested. Just make sure to get the right permissions.

Also, the right use of animation and appropriate music can draw people's eyes and ears to your online video ads.

Once you've come up with your concepts, think about what lengths your video ads need to be to get your message across.

If you want to keep your brand top of mind with people, for example, consider making a 15-second video ad that shows your brand or product in action to increase awareness.

If you're introducing a new campaign or trying to tell a bigger brand story, a 60-second ad allows enough time to show your creative idea and create a cinematic feel that will keep audiences engaged.

The online world is ever-changing, so it's best to test different ideas, learn from mistakes, and adapt your ads, rather than trying to hit a home run immediately.

Some features, like YouTube's TrueView, allow you to do live testing of different ad variations so you can play around with music, logo placement, and animation to improve your ads.

This type of iteration and testing allows you to push your creative juices to the limit and experiment with new concepts, interactions, and tactics.

Also, data analytics on online video ads let you test whether or not your messaging is resonating with your audience. This can help you do a better job targeting them, which can increase your return on investment (ROI).

Mondelēz International teamed up with ad agency Droga5 to test 3 versions of a Honey Maid online video ad. Their goal was to find the one that performed best.

All 3 ads told the story of a Hispanic family, focusing on their immigrant experience in America. But, one version was 15 seconds, the other 30 seconds, and the last 2 minutes long.

Mondelēz International made sure each version of the video ad had different balances of story, product, and messaging. Then they tested all 3 versions on YouTube.

Mondelēz International measured which version people chose to watch, how long they watched each version, and how that impacted brand favorability and awareness.

The 2-minute and the 30-second ads not only had stronger VTRs (AKA view through rates), but were also both more effective in lifting brand favorability for the brand.

KEY TAKEAWAYS

1. Online video ads can work better than TV ads because they let people view, interact, and take action.

2. Being clear about your goals help you figure out the emotions you want your ads to evoke, and what actions you want viewers to take.

3. To improve the results from your online video ads, test different creative iterations, adapt, and run the ad that performs best.

Liven Up Your Video Marketing with Live Streaming

What is live streaming?

What type of live streaming videos can help my business?

How do I set up a live streaming event?

Imagine Annisa just moved into a new home. She's purchased furniture and decorations for it, but she's missing something major – kitchen supplies.

At first, Annisa thinks, "A fork is a fork is a fork." But then she considers how much time she's spent on the rest of the items in her house, and decides to pay more attention to what brand of kitchenware she'll buy.

Annisa has a lot of different brands she can choose from, however. And to her eyes, many of them seem the same. In the end, she finds a brand that she feels good about buying.

What helped Annisa decide?

Annisa experienced live streaming, which is the use of high definition (HD) cameras and Internet connections to share live video with an audience.

By casting live streaming videos from your website, blog, or social media accounts, you can keep your audience interacting and connecting with your brand even when they aren't thinking about buying your products or services.

This continued engagement can make your brand more likable and attractive to your audience (AKA raise your brand affinity), and encourage them to give you more business in the future.

Live streaming can also be a great partner to your other video marketing efforts, and help your email marketing by getting you more signups.

LISTEN UP

How can you help make sure your livestream videos are something people will actually watch?

By live streaming content that is authentic, unique, valuable, and/or interactive.

The trick to being authentic is staying true to your brand identity and not using your livestreams as a way to sell to your audience.

Remember, live streaming isn't about making conversions right now, but instead about raising awareness of your brand and having a conversation with people. This is the moment you can share your brand's heart and soul.

Live streaming is a great opportunity to go behind the scenes of your business. You can give your audience a glimpse into how your products are made, and put a real human face to your brand by introducing the people that work with you.

Yes, you could do the same thing with a pre-recorded and slickly-produced video. But the "live" part of live streaming lets your audience know you haven't done any tricky edits, giving your story a more open and honest feel.

People also like experiences that make them feel special or benefit them. So, you can capture their attention with unique and/or valuable live streaming videos.

Often, people tuning in to watch your livestreams are some of your most loyal fans. You can reward their devotion with unique, exclusive content that they normally couldn't access or find anywhere else.

For example, you can livestream sneak peaks of new products, talks, interviews, or "invite-only" events like product launches or expos.

If you want to add value to your livestreams, try tutorials or "how-to's." Think about what type of useful guidance and knowledge your brand could authentically offer your audience.

For example, it makes sense for a kitchenware brand to livestream a chef using their products during a cooking tutorial. But it wouldn't make sense if they live streamed how-to's on home repairs, fixing cars, or becoming a street mime.

TIP

Is it really worth doing live tutorials if they're only seen once? Well, actually, anything you livestream can be used and viewed again. You can repost your live streaming videos on social media, your website, and on your blogs, and send them out in your email marketing.

Another way to get your audience involved with your livestreams is to make them interactive. This is a great way for your brand to start conversations with people.

Many live streaming providers offer a live chat option. This lets your audience ask questions, leave comments, and give feedback as they're watching your livestream.

Make sure your brand is responding to these questions and comments as they come in. Have someone who isn't starring in your livestream monitor the chat. It's hard to be in front of the camera and dealing with a live chat at the same time.

Coming up with a great content idea is just the first step to a successful live streaming event. You also need to do some planning to avoid any on-air disasters.

First, do a trial run of the livestream. This will help you see what type of unplanned issues pop up, how the process can run smoother, which elements were particularly challenging, etc.

Next, test your equipment and connections. Make sure you'll be live streaming high quality video with no blurry images, lagging, or choppiness. Start by making sure you have an HD camera (which can even be on a phone).

Take steps to ensure the video is steady and not shaky, and that your Internet connection is strong and can handle high quality video. Also, think about the lighting and backdrop. Test how visually appealing they'll be for viewers.

Finally, find the right place online to host your livestream. Many social media and video platforms like Twitter and YouTube host livestreams, but you can also embed your livestream on your site (on a dedicated landing page, for example).

One reason to livestream on your own site is to get more visitors who are then one step closer to becoming customers. You can also make strategic marketing moves, like asking people to sign up for your email list to watch your content.

TOOLS

Depending on which live streaming service you're using, you might need to get software like Adobe Flash Media Live Converter. It helps you convert your video file as it's being transferred from your camera to the service that's beaming it out to your audience.

Along with planning your actual live streaming event, figure out how you'll promote it beforehand and how you'll measure its success afterwards.

Promote your live streaming event just like you would promote an in-person event. Make your event part of your social media strategy and content calendar, and hype it on social media, on your blogs and website, and in emails.

Create a dedicated landing page on your site that lets people sign up for your live streaming event reminders. This allows you to email them the day of your event (or even a few days before), and also helps you build up your email list.

After the event, look at your metrics to gauge success. Track how many viewers, comments, and questions you received, and how many times your livestream link was shared (and on which specific social media channels).

Measure interactions (likes, reactions, etc.) and impressions, how many new emails were added to your list thanks to your event, and the amount of conversions that resulted from livestream site visitors.

Also, don't forget to keep tracking your views after the event is over and you've reposted the video of your livestream on various channels.

KEY TAKEAWAYS

1. Live streaming is an event that uses HD cameras and Internet connections to share live videos with an audience.

2. Live streaming content that is authentic, unique, valuable, and/or interactive can engage your audience and boost your audience and boost brand affinity.

3. Plan your livestream carefully, and make sure to promote it beforehand and measure its success after

Actionable Online Videos: Get More Than Views

Why should I create actionable online videos?

How is online video marketing similar to social media marketing?

How can I get more conversations, connections, and conversions from my videos?

Imagine Barry's Blossoms is a flower shop known for innovative flower arrangements and bouquets.

To reach more customers, Barry decides to create an online videos series that gives flower arranging tips and tricks – featuring the best blooms from his shop, of course.

Barry finds an online video platform that's popular with his customer base, creates a channel for his brand, and uploads his videos to it. That's all he can do, right?

Actually, Barry should change the way he thinks about video marketing.

To create videos that encourage your audience to take action, you need to get your mind into action mode.

That starts with how you view your online video channels. Instead of thinking of them as just a place to host your videos, think of them as social media platforms.

And just like your other social media marketing efforts, your video channels need to work hard to build followers (AKA subscribers), shares, likes, and comments.

Why do any of this? Because studies show that customers who engage with brands on social media are more loyal and spend up to 40% more with those brands than other customers do.

LISTEN UP

The most actionable and successful videos lead to the 3 C's we mentioned earlier: conversations, connections, and conversions.

We'll show you how you can help make sure your video marketing is worthy of all 3.

You can start conversations by describing and presenting your videos in engaging ways.

Asking questions in your video's description text can encourage viewers to respond via comments. For example, Barry's description might say, "This is a Spring bouquet with lilacs. What flowers would you like to see in my next video?"

Remember that only the first few description lines are visible before people have to click to read more, so ask your questions early. Keep them open-ended, broad (avoid any that will result in just yes or no answers), positive, and upbeat.

When people comment and respond to your questions, create a 2-way conversation by replying back. This helps both the commenters and those reading the comments know you care about your audience's thoughts and opinions.

You can also present your videos in a way that will spark more conversations – like creating playlists (AKA groupings of different videos). When one video in your playlist ends, the next one automatically starts.

Instead of sending people to a single video, you can share a link to your playlist. This raises the likelihood that they'll watch multiple videos, which can get you more engagement and more opportunities for comments and conversations.

Along with conversations, your video marketing can form long-lasting connections with your audience by turning them into subscribers.

When someone subscribes to your brand channel, they'll be notified anytime you post more content. This can help boost views and engagement levels on any new videos you share.

Some video platforms like YouTube let you put a logo or brand watermark on all your videos, which serves as a type of subscription button. It stays up while a video plays and viewers can click on it to automatically subscribe to your channel.

Adding calls to action (CTAs) in your videos can also help you get more subscribers. Your videos' voiceovers can ask viewers to subscribe, like, share, and comment, and then reiterate these requests with visual CTAs via images and text.

Of course, you can have the most persuasive CTAs in the world, but it won't matter if your audience thinks your video content is useless or boring. So, it's important to provide valuable, entertaining videos that will inspire subscribers.

And now for the last, but definitely not least, C: conversions. Let's see how your videos can turn casual viewers into customers.

You can use shortened URL's in your video description text that will direct people to your brand website for information or to make a purchase, or lead them to your app store landing page so they can download your app.

Make sure these links and your video's CTAs send people to the same location. Also, just as you did with your questions that start conversations, keep these links at the start of the video description so they're visible before the cut-off point.

TOOLS

You can also monitor how many clicks your links are generating by creating a UTM link. It's a custom URL that lets you easily track performance. You can set it up through Google Analytics.

Certain video platforms let you add interactive elements to your videos that can help drive conversions, too.

YouTube has a feature called "cards," which are video overlays that can include photos, CTA buttons, or simple text. To encourage more conversions, you can have them lead to your brand site or your app store landing page.

While you can have these cards appear at any time in your video, you should be strategic about it. Time them to happen at moments that will get you the most clicks.

For example, beauty retailer Sephora created a series of makeup tutorial videos. Anytime one of the videos introduced a new beauty product, a corresponding card popped up with the product's name and a "Buy Now" button.

KEY TAKEAWAYS

1. While views on your online videos are important, you can get even more engagement by making your videos actionable.

2. Like social media marketing, your videos and brand channel should work hard to encourage shares, likes, comments, and subscribers.

3. Start conversations by asking your audience questions, create connections via subscriptions, and drive conversations with links and interactive elements.

Weyk Global Leadership

Zachary Lukasiewicz is the Managing Director of Weyk Global. Originally from Omaha, Nebraska and attended Drake University in Des Moines, Iowa. He served as a tri-chair for the Human Capital committee of Capital Crossroads, the 10-year plan for Central Iowa, where he focused on the attraction and retention of Des Moines residents from cradle to career.

Zachary has operated 50+ accelerator assistance programs and in-house workshops, and staffed marketing teams around the globe. His focus is marketing investment - sourcing the best talent, recruiting domain experts and executing on his proven playbook and delivering the best possible experience. He sets the strategic direction and client profile within the program, including a curated team of mentors, investors and business advisors.

Zachary is responsible for making the initial relationships. He takes overall ownership of each programs' success and partners with other operations units external to Weyk Global to ensure exceptional delivery of exceptional marketing programs, and is ultimately responsible for turning good companies into great ones.

Additional:

- Builds systems around market research and data-driven management - especially in budget allocation, paid/organic, and navigating complex customer cadences.

- Experience building marketing infrastructure and communication processes throughout US Techstars' classes, reducing acquisition costs with greater capacity and cost-effectiveness

- A recognized expert on US social media in real estate, education, and human resources industries

- A leader with proven skills working with innovative teams to build customer consensus and drive buy-in behavior across purpose-driven organizations

- Motivates large organizations and individual personnel to award-winning performance and achievement

- Leadership experience encompasses direct management of 20+ personnel, over $8.5 million in assets/budgets with a record of five enterprise acquisitions and assisting in seven fundraising rounds

Zachary has served as a management consultant with startups backed by White Star Capital, Hoxton Ventures, Bloomberg Beta, Real Ventures, BDC Capital, Chris Anderson. Eduardo Gentil, Jacqueline Novogratz, Mehdi Alhassani, Ana Carolina, Entrepreneur, Obvious Ventures, MIT, Ittleson Foundation, J.M.Kaplan Fund, SC/E, MassCEC, WhiteHouse.gov, ServiceCorps, The One Foundation, The Godley Family Foundation, the Boston Foundation, Boris Jabes, Ilya Sukhar, Chris DeVore, Alex Payne, DJF, Liquid 2 Ventures, GSF, Sanjay Jain, Felix Anthony, Uma Raghavan, and TiE LaunchPad. Zachary's early experience comes from working under business leaders at market-leading companies including ISoft Data Systems, LukeUSA, AlphaPrep.net, Staffing Nerd, Immun.io, Reflect.io, Validated.co, Shaun White Enterprises, Solstice.us, Swym, Staffing Robot, Hatchlings, Coaching Actuaries, 8 to Great, Target, Paylease, MidAmerican Energy, and R&R Realty Group.

List of Books in Series

- Brand Building: Discover How to Choose a Strong Business Name, Develop Your Brand Identity, and more

- Startup: Growth Hacking, Prototyping, Crowdfunding, and Other Startup Tactics

- Social Media: How to Create Social Ads, Work with Influencers, and more

- Business Management: Lessons on Leadership, Work-Life Balance, Hiring a Team, and more

- Digital Marketing 1: How to Market Your Business Online

- Digital Marketing 2: Take Your Online Marketing to the Next Level

- Email Marketing: How to Build an Email List, Use Email Automation, Avoid Spam Filters, and more

- Business Insights: Get to Know Your Audience: Lessons on User Testing, Research, and Customer Insights

- Mobile Marketing: Engaging Your Target Audience on Their Mobile Phones

- Content Marketing: Planning, Creating, and Sharing Compelling Content

- Video Marketing: Creating Actionable Online Videos, Hardworking Video Ads, and more

- Analytics: Lessons on Digital Metrics, Google Analytics, and more

- User Experience: Helping Users Get the Most out of your Website, Mobile Store, Apps, and more

- Websites: Tips on Creating a Business that Appeals to Customers

- Business Planning: Learn How to Start a Business and Set It Up for Success

- Customer Engagement: Learn How to Create Your Business Story and Find Your Target Audience